Cover Me Movement Challenge

10 Week Small Group Study Guide

Dr. Mark A. Smith

ISBN:978-0-9661709-5-5

DEDICATION

At the time of the first release of this publication, the world in general and the United States in particular faces struggles internally. This manual is dedicated to all those who openly and willingly embrace the desire and effort to change the world, by changing their community by changing – themselves.

If we are willing to turn to God every day and ask how we can better love our neighbors, we have a chance. And as my friend and associate Kenneth Brandy says, "I woke up with a chance."

To God be the glory!

Cover Me Movement
<u>Edition</u>

Join us!

We the people can change the world!

www.CoverMeMovement.com

CONTENTS

SPECIAL THANKS

In this edition, we just wanted to give a
Special Thanks
to our
Sponsor.

Without them this would not have been possible.
Please check them out on the web :

https://cutt.ly/HappyCoffee

And one last thing, we will be mounting a campaign
to get our friend, Jaci Velasquez,
recognition for her work on the title song, "Cover Me".

Our goal is to get her a Gold Record!
More information will be available by
September 4, 2020
And will be available at

www.Gold4Jaci.com

Check it out beginning September 4th!

ACKNOWLEDGMENTS

There are so many people and organizations that have influenced this effort. First, I want to say thank you to Kenneth Brandy, who was brave enough to embrace the dream of a free America with me. Thank you to Craig Wallin who made it possible in a pandemic world for the movie to have an outdoor World Premiere. To all my friends who put in funds to make the movie possible, thank you. And to my friend Kevin Plank who endured my lack of music knowledge initially and co-wrote the songs with me, thank you.

I must also Thank Jaci Velasquez and her team for the remix of the song, Cover Me in English and Cúbreme in Spanish.

And to Danny Trejo who planted the seeds for me about taking life in steps.

CHAPTER 1
THE SONG – PART ONE

Welcome to the beginning of our journey in the Cover Me Movement! As we begin our journey together, it is important to understand what the Cover Me Movement is, what this manual is about, and what we will be doing the over this time we have together.

THE MOVEMENT

The Cover Me Movement began from two people with a desire to make a difference in our world. Kenneth Brandy, my friend, and I wanted to not just watch as the world around us and the people in it struggled to deal with each other as fellow human beings. We started with the song that Jaci Velasquez had remixed – Cover Me – for the movie by the same name in which she had a role. That grew into a week-long series of interviews that drew a large amount of attention, which lead to the request to focus on the idea expressed in the Song, Book, and Movie. That theme is "the hope of perfect love" which I suggest is in every human being. To get that message out, the Movement was born and thus this manual.

THE MANUAL

This Manual is created to have an impact on those that use it. What it is NOT is some great reading material for an intellectual read near the fireplace on a cold winter's night. This Manual is meant to be a practical guide on our journey. To that end it is laid out in the order that we will follow over a scheduled 10-week period. Week 1 is the introduction and explanation of how we will proceed. We will also begin our conversation about the song. Weeks 2, 3, 4, and 5 will be about the movie. Weeks 6, 7, 8, and 9 will be about the book. Week 10 we will revisit the song and wrap up our time together. More about that in a minute.

This manual is laid out to help us become involved in the actual subject of that week itself, and then tie the weeks together. Because it is a Study Guide, it does just that – guides us through the study of materials. It is laid out to help us take some information from the topic, examine it, interact with it, and create something useful from it.

In my previous work as a consultant to business, I developed a process that helped the average individual accelerate both what they learned and the resulting action they took. We will be using that format here. The manual is laid out so that the first part of each week addresses the subject matter. The last five pages for each week are used to create a Living Journal that ties our thoughts each week to our actions during the week that become a portion of the next week's review. There is a page specifically for Notes. Since this is a Living Journal, you can of course make notes anywhere. The last four pages of each chapter for each week are key. They are titled Activity, Accomplishment, Awareness, and Alignment. This is how we tie our thoughts and hopes to actions and reflections.

WEEKLY GROUP

Our overall effort is focused on what I suggest are the focal points of the Gospel, FP1 and FP2. Focal Point 1 – Love God with all your heart, soul, and mind. Focal Point 2 – Love your neighbor as yourself. After this week, we will begin each meeting with a brief review of how we did during the week. Each week's topic will be introduced and discussed from our own perspective. Scriptures will be introduced by each person that wants to contribute their favorite on the topic. We want to tie these together and think about how we can apply them to ourselves – FP1 – as well as share them in a helpful way with others – FP2.

On the Activity page we will do our best to list an FP1 and an FP2 for each thing we discuss. This becomes our plan. Then each day during the week we look at these for a few minutes to see if we can implement one that day. When we do, we record that on the Accomplishment page. What did we become either more aware of or newly aware of as a result of recording our Accomplishment? Write that one the Awareness page. Then either at that time or sometime during the week review the Awareness entries and determine if there is something from these that we want to hold as valuable, something we want to strive towards doing or becoming on a regular basis. This is something we record on the Alignment page.

When we come back to the group the next week, we will share some of our notes and experiences with each other in our review time. Then we will repeat the process with the topic for that week.

Each meeting will be divided up into learning segments. This means we will take at least one break in the middle of the meeting, and up to four breaks overall. We do this because the mind cannot absorb material well for an hour-long period. Somewhere between 10 and 20 minutes our minds will begin to drift. Therefore, we will take breaks. Great! Let's get started.

WEEK 1 – THE SONG PART ONE
Let's listen to the lyric video, "Cover Me" by Jaci Velasquez from YouTube. Be sure to watch the words on the screen.

What were some of your reactions to the song and lyrics?

What does "the hope of perfect love" mean to you?

Let's briefly review the story of Ruth and Boaz. What do we know?

Let's revisit the song and see if we see anything different now that we have the story of Ruth and Boaz to compare to it.

How does the story of Ruth and Boaz tie to the song for you?

What was the hope of perfect love to Boaz?

What was the hope of perfect love to Ruth?

How does the story of Ruth and Boaz apply to each of us as believers?

Considering Ruth and Boaz, and our FP1, are there one or more Activities that we can plan for the coming week that could help us experience the hope of perfect love? Write those as FP1 – and then whatever it is on the Activity page in this chapter.

Again, considering the story of Ruth and Boaz, and now our FP2, are there one or more Activities that we can plan for the coming week that could help us to help others to experience the hope of perfect love? Write those as FP2 – and then whatever it is on the Activity page in this chapter.

It is important to note here that this is not some dissertation we are writing. Not a novel, or a play. This is our Living Journal that we use to tie each week's topic to something practical in our life. There is no test. No reward for getting something "right" or penalty for getting something "wrong".

There is evidence that shows when we write something down, and then reread it later, it has greater impact on us than something typewritten. There are at least a couple reasons for this. One is it takes a different set of neurons and muscles to write than to type. Second, we recognize our own writing. When we come back to it later, seeing our handwriting brings the memories with it. We tie the same feelings and emotions to the words we recognize as our own.

Okay, we will just wrap up with a couple thoughts about music and song. Then let's discuss what we have written. If there are any closing thoughts, please share.

Remember this week to watch the lyric video at least once, and preferably once each day.

Thant's it! See you next week!

Notes:

Li4.MS Category
Activity

Li4.MS Category

Accomplishment

Li4.MS Category

Awareness

Li4.MS Category
Alignment

CHAPTER 2
THE MOVIE – PART ONE

This week we begin to look at the movie, "Cover Me". We do this with the same mindset we learned from the introduction to the Song. We are looking for "the hope of perfect love" in the story. We want to learn about this family and see what we can take away into our own lives.

WEEK 2 – THE MOVIE PART ONE

Remembering that this is a Study Guide with the goal of applying what we learn to our lives, we want to revisit our process (Li4.MS) from last week. Let's see how we did.

Let's each share about the items we recorded in Activity. Anyone want to be first?

Okay, great. And how did we do with Accomplishment? Did we get it done – Yes-No-Sort of?

So, what are you Aware of now that you had that Activity planned and the result in Accomplishment? Even if we did not do it, what did "not doing it" speak to you personally?

Finally, now that you have been through that Activity, Accomplishment, Awareness cycle, is there any Alignment you want to make for yourself going forward. Just a note, we are not necessarily looking for World Peace here. Keep it simple. Maybe picture it in your mind as you write it down.

Great! Now to the movie, "Cover Me".

We will be watching until about 11:35 into the movie where Mia wakes up in bed. This part of the movie introduces to the main characters. It gives us the background set-up for the rest of the movie, and why there is a need to re-think life.

Make notes below of anything that catches your attention, especially as it relates to life and our own journey towards the hope for perfect love.

The Mysterious Stranger talking leads to a montage.

Mia drives to work and tells a story.

Coffee to work.

Meeting preparation.

Meeting presentation.

Mia confronts Richie.

Mia's dream.

So, what do you think? Is there any part of this that you can relate to in your own life?

If this brings to mind anything that you want to do as an Activity in the coming week, go ahead and record that now in the Activity section for this chapter.

Okay, that is a great start. We will now be watching from where we left off to 23:33. In this segment Mia is thinking about her business that her father left to her. She just had a dream about his death again, and she wants to make sure everything at work is okay. She says good-bye to her family to check on things and heads off for coffee – just another day. Except it isn't. She meets our Stranger – maybe? Then going to the office seems – odd. What should she do?

Again, make notes below of anything that catches your attention, especially as it relates to life and our own journey towards the hope for perfect love.

Mia makes toast and greets good morning to her family.

Mia wants coffee, but she is early.

Mia meets our Mysterious Stranger. He makes her listen to a story.

Mia wakes up – or did she? Was it a dream?

Arrives at the office, but it seems surreal.

Has a confrontation with Richie, and he expresses concern, right?

Mia reflects on life with her Dad. She decides something.

So, the plot thickens, right? Did Mia have a dream in a parking lot? Can you relate to that? Is Mia right to be concerned? What do you think of Mia and her Dad? If you were Mia, what would you do next?

Let's take that thought and what we made note of in our first segment. This week, is there anything we saw that ties to the hope of perfect love for you? If so, what Activity can you do this week to implement something about it in your life, as an FP1. If you did not have anything that you related to, what can you come up with as an Activity for implementing an FP1 this week? Let's write those down. Is there an FP2? Write that down as well. And it is okay to have more than one of each. Again, make them realistic.

Notes:

Li4.MS Category
Activity

Li4.MS Category

Accomplishment

Li4.MS Category
Awareness

Li4.MS Category
Alignment

CHAPTER 3
THE MOVIE – PART TWO

This week we continue to look at the movie, "Cover Me". We do this with the same mindset we learned from the introduction to the Song and last week's movie introduction. We are looking for "the hope of perfect love" in the story. We want to learn about this family and see what we can take away into our own lives.

WEEK 3 – THE MOVIE PART TWO

Remembering that this is a Study Guide with the goal of applying what we learn to our lives, we want to revisit our process (Li4.MS) from last week. Let's see how we did.

Let's each share about the items we recorded in Activity. Anyone want to be first?

Okay, great. And how did we do with Accomplishment? Did we get it done – Yes-No-Sort of?

So, what are you Aware of now that you had that Activity planned and the result in Accomplishment? Even if we did not do it, what did "not doing it" speak to you personally?

Finally, now that you have been through that Activity, Accomplishment, Awareness cycle, is there any Alignment you want to make for yourself going forward. Just a note, we are not necessarily looking for World Peace here. Keep it simple. Maybe picture it in your mind as you write it down.

Great! Now once again, to the movie, "Cover Me".

We will be watching from 23:33 until about 34:56 into the movie where Mia takes off to determine what is real. This part of the movie begins to develop the plot of the relationships between characters.

Make notes below of anything that catches your attention, especially as it relates to life and our own journey towards the hope for perfect love.

Meet Jacob and Benny.

Benny and Mia review the "Loyalty Clause".

Benny reveals Mia's inheritance.

Tea Party and a bad omen.

So, what do you think? Is there any part of this that you can relate to in your own life?

If this brings to mind anything that you want to do as an Activity in the coming week, go ahead and record that now in the Activity section for this chapter.

Okay, that is a great start. We will now be watching from where we left off to 43:33. In this segment the Old Man's stories begin to become true in Mia's life. Benny provides a warning, and things take strange twists at work. What should Mia do? What would you do if it was you?

Again, make notes below of anything that catches your attention, especially as it relates to life and our own journey towards the hope for perfect love.

Old Man's prophecies begin to come true.

Card declined.

Changes at work.

Benny calls with a warning.

Breaking in.

Escorted out.

So, now things are getting REAL interesting. Did the Old Man know all this would happen? Is Benny right to be concerned? And why is work changing?

Let's take that thought and what we made note of in our Notes segment. This week, is there anything we saw that ties to the hope of perfect love for you? If so, what Activity can you do this week to implement something about it in your life, as an FP1. If you did not have anything that you related to, what can you come up with as an Activity for implementing an FP1 this week? Let's write those down. Is there an FP2? Write that down as well. And it is okay to have more than one of each. Again, make them realistic.

Notes:

Li4.MS Category
Activity

Li4.MS Category

Accomplishment

Li4.MS Category
Awareness

Li4.MS Category
Alignment

CHAPTER 4
THE MOVIE – PART THREE

This week we again continue a deeper look at the movie, "Cover Me". We want to consider how "the hope of perfect love" in the story is revealing itself. We want to compare and contrast our lives with those of the characters here to see what we can take away into our own lives.

WEEK 4 – THE MOVIE PART THREE

Remembering that this is a Study Guide with the goal of applying what we learn to our lives, we want to revisit our process (Li4.MS) from last week. Let's see how we did.

Let's each share about the items we recorded in Activity. Anyone want to be first?

Okay, great. And how did we do with Accomplishment? Did we get it done – Yes-No-Sort of?

So, what are you Aware of now for which you had an Activity planned and the result in Accomplishment? Even if we did not do it, what did "not doing it" speak to you personally?

Finally, now that you have been through that Activity, Accomplishment, Awareness cycle, is there any Alignment you want to make for yourself going forward. Again, simple is good. Keep it simple. Maybe picture it in your mind as you write it down.

Great! Now to the movie, "Cover Me".

We will be watching from about 43:31 into the movie where Mo and Leanne confront Mia in the parking lot till 57:54 where Mia, Mom, and Robert work through some of their past. This segment of our study looks at what is the mystery and maybe corruption that is in place.

Make notes below of anything that catches your attention, especially as it relates to life and our own journey towards the hope for perfect love.

Mo and Leanne confront Mia and form a team.

Officer Jordan and Mo face off.

Garbage can trick play.

Leanne and Mia celebrate the small victory.

Mia confronts Richie in the scam.

Mia calls mom from jail for help.

Mia in jail cell with unusual company.

Mia bonded out.

Mia, Mom, and Robert confront the past.

So, what do you think? How did the Old Man get into the women's holding tank? How did he leave? And isn't it hard to confront a misjudgment of others from the past? Is there any part of this that you can relate to in your own life?

If this brings to mind anything that you want to do as an Activity in the coming week, go ahead and record that now in the Activity section for this chapter.

Okay, that is a great start. We will now be watching from where we left off to 1:06:53. Mia, Mom, and Robert go to Benny's to hear about the way out. Sadly, no money. Mia and Benny talk, and Mia drives home in the RV, reflecting on life.

Again, make notes below of anything that catches your attention, especially as it relates to life and our own journey towards the hope for perfect love.

Drive to Benny's.

Benny explains a possible way out, with a catch.

Benny and Mia have a heart to heart.

Mia reflects on her life and what the Old Man told her as she drives home from Benny's in an RV.

So many twists! Benny has an almost solution. Benny and Mia both have issues about their fathers. And then she gets to think through all of the pieces with no answer in sight. Does this sound similar to anything in your own life? If you were Mia, what would you do next?

Let's take that thought and what we made note of in our first segment. This week, is there anything we saw that ties to the hope of perfect love for you? If so, what Activity can you do this week to implement something about it in your life, as an FP1. If you did not have anything that you related to, what can you come up with as an Activity for implementing an FP1 this week? Let's write those down. Is there an FP2? Write that down as well. And it is okay to have more than one of each. Again, make them realistic.

Notes:

Li4.MS Category

Activity

Li4.MS Category

Accomplishment

Li4.MS Category
Awareness

Li4.MS Category
Alignment

CHAPTER 5
THE MOVIE – PART FOUR

This week we wrap up our movie review. The movie, "Cover Me" has given us a chance to look at the life of someone that is caught up in life's complexities, trying to find their way. Sound familiar? We are looking for "the hope of perfect love" in the story. We want to learn about how this family resolves some amazing challenges in the face of no answer.

WEEK 5 – THE MOVIE PART FOUR

Remembering that this is a Study Guide with the goal of applying what we learn to our lives, we want to revisit our process (Li4.MS) from last week. Let's see how we did.

Let's each share about the items we recorded in Activity. Anyone want to be first?

Okay, great. And how did we do with Accomplishment? Did we get it done – Yes-No-Sort of?

So, what are you Aware of now that you had that Activity planned and the result in Accomplishment? Even if we did not do it, what did "not doing it" speak to you personally?

Finally, now that you have been through that Activity, Accomplishment, Awareness cycle, is there any Alignment you want to make for yourself going forward. Maybe picture it in your mind as you write it down.

Great! Now to the wrap up the movie, "Cover Me".

We will be watching from 1:06:53 until about 1:17:40 into the movie where Mia has her life flash before her eyes. This part of the movie makes us feel all is lost. We see what looks like a situation where the bad guys will win.

Make notes below of anything that catches your attention, especially as it relates to life and our own journey towards the hope for perfect love.

Mia and Kevin argue.

Mia and Kevin reconcile and question angels.

Bag of cash and a stranger.

Kevin sends Mia to save the company.

Mia gives Luisa instructions en route.

The March to…

Elevator ride.

Race against time.

The gang confronts Richie and his accomplice.

Richie pulls a gun and they argue.

The tackle and a shot fired!

Mia's life flashes before her eyes.

So, what do you think? Is there any part of this that you can relate to in your own life? Have you ever had a near tragic moment that made you rethink life?

If this brings to mind anything that you want to do as an Activity in the coming week, go ahead and record that now in the Activity section for this chapter.

Okay, that is a great start. We will now be watching from where we left off to the end. In this segment Mia is miraculously saved from the bullet. Then she gives a gift to her employees and one gets promoted. Richie meets the Old Man. Mia and her family finally spend the time together to enjoy themselves.

Again, make notes below of anything that catches your attention, especially as it relates to life and our own journey towards the hope for perfect love.

Saved from a bullet.

New partners and Richie escorted out.

Luisa promoted.

Richie meets the Old Man.

New boss still with family traditions.

Wake up to breakfast in bed.

New plan?

Mia pulls the pieces together for a better life.

Cover Me by Jaci Velasquez and the credits roll.

So, what did you think? Have you ever had a "visit" from God or an angel, encouraging you to change? How did it go?

Let's take that thought and what we made note of in our first

segment. This week, is there anything we saw that ties to the hope of perfect love for you? If so, what Activity can you do this week to implement something about it in your life, as an FP1. If you did not have anything that you related to, what can you come up with as an Activity for implementing an FP1 this week? Let's write those down. Is there an FP2? Write that down as well. And it is okay to have more than one of each. Again, make them realistic.

Notes:

Li4.MS Category

Activity

Li4.MS Category

Accomplishment

Li4.MS Category

Awareness

Li4.MS Category

Alignment

CHAPTER 6
THE BOOK – PART ONE

This week we begin to look at the book, "Cover Me". Keep in mind that movies adapted from a book to the screen are seldom ever like the book exactly, and "Cover Me" was no different. To reach an even broader audience with the movie, we switched the roles of the husband and wife with regard to who works at home and who goes into an office. We do this book review with the same mindset we learned from the introduction to the Song and the review of the movie. We are looking for "the hope of perfect love" in the story. We want to learn about this family and see what we can take away into our own lives.

WEEK 6 – THE BOOK PART ONE
Remembering that this is a Study Guide with the goal of applying what we learn to our lives, we want to revisit our process (Li4.MS) from last week. Let's see how we did.

Let's each share about the items we recorded in Activity. Anyone want to be first?

Okay, great. And how did we do with Accomplishment? Did we get it done – Yes-No-Sort of?

So, what are you Aware of now that you had that Activity planned and the result in Accomplishment? Even if we did not do it, what did "not doing it" speak to you personally?

Finally, now that you have been through that Activity, Accomplishment, Awareness cycle, is there any Alignment you want to make for yourself going forward. Keep it simple. Maybe picture it in your mind as you write it down.

Great! Now to the book, "Cover Me".

We will be reviewing chapters numbered 1-4, and the Prologue, when we meet. Be sure to read these ahead of time and record your responses to the questions here. It is these questions that we will be discussing when we meet. This will be a little different from the movie as we will not be actually watching something. If anyone has a passage they would like us to read out loud, then let's do that. It is a great way to show how we interpret what is being said.

Make notes below of anything that catches your attention, especially as it relates to life and our own journey towards the hope for perfect love.

PROLOGUE
ANSWER BEFORE WE MEET
What is the overall tone you pick up from this segment?

Record the relationships you see. What do we learn from the characters about these relationships?

What do you think about the night shirt? The Poem?

Does reading this segment make you want to read more of the book?

What do you think the characters are thinking about the hope of perfect love, if anything, as this segment ends?

DISCUSS AND WRITE RESPONSES DURING MEEETING

So, what did you think? Have you ever had a fun moment that was unplanned? Maybe one thought out by someone else? How did it go?

Let's take that thought and what we made note of in our first segment. This week, is there anything we saw that ties to the hope of perfect love for you? If so, what Activity can you do this week to implement something about it in your life, as an FP1. If you did not have anything that you related to, what can you come up with as an Activity for implementing an FP1 this week? Let's write those down. Is there an FP2? Write that down as well. And it is okay to have more than one of each. Again, make them realistic.

Make notes below of anything that catches your attention, especially as it relates to life and our own journey towards the hope for perfect love.

CHAPER 1 – The Drive To Work
ANSWER BEFORE WE MEET
What is the overall tone you pick up from this segment?

Record the relationships you see. What do we learn from the characters about these relationships?

What do you think about the "auto-pilot"? The memory of his dad?

Does reading this segment make you want to read more of the book?

What do you think the characters are thinking about the hope of perfect love, if anything, as this segment ends?

DISCUSS AND WRITE RESPONSES DURING MEEETING

So, what did you think? Is this a life you would want? Is it anything like the life you have now? Did you ever have an experience where you "suddenly arrived"? How did it go?

Let's take that thought and what we made note of in our first

segment. This week, is there anything we saw that ties to the hope of perfect love for you? If so, what Activity can you do this week to implement something about it in your life, as an FP1. If you did not have anything that you related to, what can you come up with as an Activity for implementing an FP1 this week? Let's write those down. Is there an FP2? Write that down as well. And it is okay to have more than one of each. Again, make them realistic.

Make notes below of anything that catches your attention, especially as it relates to life and our own journey towards the hope for perfect love.

CHAPER 2 – First Meeting
ANSWER BEFORE WE MEET
What is the overall tone you pick up from this segment?

Record the relationships you see. What do we learn from the characters about these relationships?

What do you think about the new acquaintance of Michael – the Old Man?

Does reading this segment make you want to read more of the book?

What do you think the characters are thinking about the hope of perfect love, if anything, as this segment ends?

DISCUSS AND WRITE RESPONSES DURING MEEETING

So, what did you think? Is this a life you would want? Is it anything like the life you have now? Did you ever have an experience where you met someone, and it went a little odd? How did it go?
Let's take that thought and what we made note of in our first segment. This week, is there anything we saw that ties to the hope of perfect love for you? If so, what Activity can you do this week to implement something about it in your life, as an FP1. If you did not have anything that you related to, what can you come up with as an

Activity for implementing an FP1 this week? Let's write those down. Is there an FP2? Write that down as well. And it is okay to have more than one of each. Again, make them realistic.

Make notes below of anything that catches your attention, especially as it relates to life and our own journey towards the hope for perfect love.

CHAPER 3 – Assumptions – What Is It That They Say?
ANSWER BEFORE WE MEET
What is the overall tone you pick up from this segment?

Record the relationships you see. What do we learn from the characters about these relationships?

What do you think about the assumptions Michael makes about the Old Man?

Does reading this segment make you want to read more of the book?

What do you think the characters are thinking about the hope of perfect love, if anything, as this segment ends?

DISCUSS AND WRITE RESPONSES DURING MEEETING

So, what did you think? Is this a life you would want? Is it anything like the life you have now? Did you ever have an experience where you made an assumption and then discovered it may not be quite right? How did it go?

Let's take that thought and what we made note of in our first segment. This week, is there anything we saw that ties to the hope of perfect love for you? If so, what Activity can you do this week to implement something about it in your life, as an FP1. If you did not have anything that you related to, what can you come up with as an Activity for implementing an FP1 this week? Let's write those down. Is there an FP2? Write that down as well. And it is okay to have more than one of each. Again, make them realistic.

Make notes below of anything that catches your attention, especially as it relates to life and our own journey towards the hope for perfect love.

CHAPER 4 – The Journey Home
ANSWER BEFORE WE MEET
What is the overall tone you pick up from this segment?

Record the relationships you see. What do we learn from the characters about these relationships?

What do you think about Michael's sense of the location being strange?

Does reading this segment make you want to read more of the book?

What do you think the characters are thinking about the hope of perfect love, if anything, as this segment ends?

DISCUSS AND WRITE RESPONSES DURING MEEETING

So, what did you think? Would you like an encounter like this? Did you ever have an experience where something seemed odd about time and distance?   How did it go?
Let's take that thought and what we made note of in our first segment. This week, is there anything we saw that ties to the hope of perfect love for you? If so, what Activity can you do this week to implement something about it in your life, as an FP1. If you did not have anything that you related to, what can you come up with as an Activity for implementing an FP1 this week? Let's write those down. Is there an FP2? Write that down as well. And it is okay to have more than one of each. Again, make them realistic.

Notes:

Li4.MS Category

Activity

Li4.MS Category

Accomplishment

Li4.MS Category

Awareness

Li4.MS Category

Alignment

CHAPTER 7
THE BOOK – PART TWO

This week we continue to look at the book, "Cover Me". Keep in mind that books adapted to the screen are seldom ever like the book exactly "Cover Me" was no different. Each week we will see more and more differences, and yet similarities. We do this book review with the same mindset we learned from the introduction to the Song and the review of the movie. We are looking for "the hope of perfect love" in the story. We want to learn about this family and see what we can take away into our own lives.

WEEK 7 – THE BOOK PART TWO
Remembering that this is a Study Guide with the goal of applying what we learn to our lives, we want to revisit our process (Li4.MS) from last week. Let's see how we did.

Let's each share about the items we recorded in Activity. Anyone want to be first?

Okay, great. And how did we do with Accomplishment? Did we get it done – Yes-No-Sort of?

So, what are you Aware of now that you had that Activity planned and the result in Accomplishment? Even if we did not do it, what did "not doing it" speak to you personally?

Finally, now that you have been through that Activity, Accomplishment, Awareness cycle, is there any Alignment you want to make for yourself going forward. Keep it simple. Maybe picture it in your mind as you write it down.

Great! Now to the book, "Cover Me".

We will be reviewing chapters numbered 5-8, when we meet. Be sure to read these ahead of time and record your responses to the questions here. It is these questions that we will be discussing when we meet. Again, this will be a little different from the movie as we will not be actually watching something. If anyone has a passage they would like us to read out loud, then let's do that. It is a great way to show how we interpret what is being said.

Make notes below of anything that catches your attention, especially as it relates to life and our own journey towards the hope for perfect love.

CHAPER 5 – Room For Living
ANSWER BEFORE WE MEET
What is the overall tone you pick up from this segment?

Record the relationships you see. What do we learn from the characters about these relationships?

What do you think of the many notebooks Michael finds?

Does reading this segment make you want to read more of the book?

What do you think the characters are thinking about the hope of perfect love, if anything, as this segment ends?

DISCUSS AND WRITE RESPONSES DURING MEEETING

So, what did you think? Is this a life you would want? Is it anything like the life you have now? Did you ever have an experience where you find that someone has something they do profusely but you had no idea? How did impact you?

Let's take that thought and what we made note of in our first segment. This week, is there anything we saw that ties to the hope of perfect love for you? If so, what Activity can you do this week to implement something about it in your life, as an FP1. If you did not have anything that you related to, what can you come up with as an Activity for implementing an FP1 this week? Let's write those down. Is there an FP2? Write that down as well. And it is okay to have more than one of each. Again, make them realistic.

Make notes below of anything that catches your attention, especially as it relates to life and our own journey towards the hope for perfect love.

CHAPER 6 – The Storyteller
ANSWER BEFORE WE MEET
What is the overall tone you pick up from this segment?

Record the relationships you see. What do we learn from the characters about these relationships?

What do you think about the Old Man's way of making the story be about Michael?

Does reading this segment make you want to read more of the book?

What do you think the characters are thinking about the hope of perfect love, if anything, as this segment ends?

DISCUSS AND WRITE RESPONSES DURING MEEETING

So, what did you think? Is Michael's life one you would want? Is it anything like the life you have now? Did you ever have an experience where talking to someone they were asking you questions and concerned about you? How did it go?

Let's take that thought and what we made note of in our first segment. This week, is there anything we saw that ties to the hope of perfect love for you? If so, what Activity can you do this week to implement something about it in your life, as an FP1. If you did not have anything that you related to, what can you come up with as an Activity for implementing an FP1 this week? Let's write those down. Is there an FP2? Write that down as well. And it is okay to have more than one of each. Again, make them realistic.

Make notes below of anything that catches your attention, especially as it relates to life and our own journey towards the hope for perfect love.

CHAPER 7 – The Story Unfolds
ANSWER BEFORE WE MEET
What is the overall tone you pick up from this segment?

Record the relationships you see. What do we learn from the characters about these relationships?

What do you think about box the Old Man kept hidden away?

Does reading this segment make you want to read more of the book?

What do you think the characters are thinking about the hope of perfect love, if anything, as this segment ends?

DISCUSS AND WRITE RESPONSES DURING MEEETING

So, what did you think? Do you have a treasure chest hidden away? Is Michael's experience with the Old Man anything like a relationship you have now? Did you ever have an experience where you were discussing memories with a stranger? How did it go?

Let's take that thought and what we made note of in our first segment. This week, is there anything we saw that ties to the hope of perfect love for you? If so, what Activity can you do this week to implement something about it in your life, as an FP1. If you did not have anything that you related to, what can you come up with as an Activity for implementing an FP1 this week? Let's write those down. Is there an FP2? Write that down as well. And it is okay to have more than one of each. Again, make them realistic.

Make notes below of anything that catches your attention, especially as it relates to life and our own journey towards the hope for perfect love.

CHAPER 8 – Betrayal And Intrigue
ANSWER BEFORE WE MEET
What is the overall tone you pick up from this segment?

Record the relationships you see. What do we learn from the characters about these relationships?

What do you think about the revelation of what happened to the Old Man, and ultimately his name?

Does reading this segment make you want to read more of the book?

What do you think the characters are thinking about the hope of perfect love, if anything, as this segment ends?

DISCUSS AND WRITE RESPONSES DURING MEEETING

So, what did you think? Would you like an encounter like this? Did you ever have an experience where something seemed odd, like you had heard or seen it before, or it so directly related to you? How did it go?

Let's take that thought and what we made note of in our first segment. This week, is there anything we saw that ties to the hope of perfect love for you? If so, what Activity can you do this week to implement something about it in your life, as an FP1. If you did not have anything that you related to, what can you come up with as an Activity for implementing an FP1 this week? Let's write those down. Is there an FP2? Write that down as well. And it is okay to have more than one of each. Again, make them realistic.

Notes:

Li4.MS Category
Activity

Li4.MS Category

Accomplishment

Li4.MS Category

Awareness

Li4.MS Category

Alignment

CHAPTER 8
THE BOOK – PART THREE

This week we continue to look at the book, "Cover Me", crossing over the mid-point. We do this book review with the same mindset we learned from the introduction to the Song and the review of the movie. We are looking for "the hope of perfect love" in the story. We want to learn about this family and see what we can take away into our own lives.

WEEK 8 – THE BOOK PART THREE
Remembering that this is a Study Guide with the goal of applying what we learn to our lives, we want to revisit our process (Li4.MS) from last week. Let's see how we did.

Let's each share about the items we recorded in Activity. Anyone want to be first?

Okay, great. And how did we do with Accomplishment? Did we get it done – Yes-No-Sort of?

So, what are you Aware of now that you had that Activity planned and the result in Accomplishment? Even if we did not do it, what did "not doing it" speak to you personally?

Finally, now that you have been through that Activity, Accomplishment, Awareness cycle, is there any Alignment you want to make for yourself going forward. Keep it simple. Maybe picture it in your mind as you write it down.

Great! Now to the book, "Cover Me".

We will be reviewing chapters numbered 8-11, when we meet. Be sure to read these ahead of time and record your responses to the questions here. It is these questions that we will be discussing when we meet. If anyone has a passage they would like us to read out loud, then let's do that. It is a great way to show how we interpret what is being said.

Make notes below of anything that catches your attention, especially as it relates to life and our own journey towards the hope for perfect love.

CHAPER 8 – Sirens Of The Morning
ANSWER BEFORE WE MEET
What is the overall tone you pick up from this segment?

Record the relationships you see. What do we learn from the characters about these relationships?

What do you think of the where Michael found himself?

Does reading this segment make you want to read more of the book?

What do you think the characters are thinking about the hope of perfect love, if anything, as this segment ends?

DISCUSS AND WRITE RESPONSES DURING MEEETING

So, what did you think? Can you relate to this experience of

Michael's? Did you ever have an experience where you find that someone what you thought you just experienced was really a dream… maybe? How did that impact you?

Let's take that thought and what we made note of in our first segment. This week, is there anything we saw that ties to the hope of perfect love for you? If so, what Activity can you do this week to implement something about it in your life, as an FP1. If you did not have anything that you related to, what can you come up with as an Activity for implementing an FP1 this week? Let's write those down. Is there an FP2? Write that down as well. And it is okay to have more than one of each. Again, make them realistic.

Make notes below of anything that catches your attention, especially as it relates to life and our own journey towards the hope for perfect love.

CHAPER 9 – Breakfast
ANSWER BEFORE WE MEET
What is the overall tone you pick up from this segment?

Record the relationships you see. What do we learn from the characters about these relationships?

What do you think about Michael's "flashbacks" to his dream?

Does reading this segment make you want to read more of the book?

What do you think the characters are thinking about the hope of perfect love, if anything, as this segment ends?

DISCUSS AND WRITE RESPONSES DURING MEEETING

So, what did you think? Is it anything like the life you have now? Did you ever have an experience where talking to someone and it seemed like the thing had already happened or you already discussed it? How did it go?

Let's take that thought and what we made note of in our first

segment. This week, is there anything we saw that ties to the hope of perfect love for you? If so, what Activity can you do this week to implement something about it in your life, as an FP1. If you did not have anything that you related to, what can you come up with as an Activity for implementing an FP1 this week? Let's write those down. Is there an FP2? Write that down as well. And it is okay to have more than one of each. Again, make them realistic.

Make notes below of anything that catches your attention, especially as it relates to life and our own journey towards the hope for perfect love.

CHAPER 10 – An Alternate Route
ANSWER BEFORE WE MEET
What is the overall tone you pick up from this segment?

Record the relationships you see. What do we learn from the characters about these relationships?

What do you think about the way that things had changed with Manny, and because of a dream?

Does reading this segment make you want to read more of the book?

What do you think the characters are thinking about the hope of perfect love, if anything, as this segment ends?

DISCUSS AND WRITE RESPONSES DURING MEEETING

So, what did you think? Did a dream you had seemed to be similar to someone else's dream? Have you ever had a dream that changed your life? How did it go?

Let's take that thought and what we made note of in our first segment. This week, is there anything we saw that ties to the hope of perfect love for you? If so, what Activity can you do this week to implement something about it in your life, as an FP1. If you did not have anything that you related to, what can you come up with as an Activity for implementing an FP1 this week? Let's write those down. Is there an FP2? Write that down as well. And it is okay to have more than one of each. Again, make them realistic.

Make notes below of anything that catches your attention, especially as it relates to life and our own journey towards the hope for perfect love.

CHAPER 11 – A Hero Revealed
ANSWER BEFORE WE MEET
What is the overall tone you pick up from this segment?

Record the relationships you see. What do we learn from the characters about these relationships?

What do you think about the revelation of the similarity between what the Old Man said and what was happening in Michael's actual life?

Does reading this segment make you want to read more of the book?

What do you think the characters are thinking about the hope of perfect love, if anything, as this segment ends?

DISCUSS AND WRITE RESPONSES DURING MEEETING

So, what did you think? Would you like an encounter like this? Did you ever have an experience where something seemed odd where you were experiencing an actual dream in real life? How did it go?

Let's take that thought and what we made note of in our first segment. This week, is there anything we saw that ties to the hope of perfect love for you? If so, what Activity can you do this week to implement something about it in your life, as an FP1. If you did not have anything that you related to, what can you come up with as an Activity for implementing an FP1 this week? Let's write those down.

Is there an FP2? Write that down as well. And it is okay to have more than one of each. Again, make them realistic.

Notes:

Li4.MS Category

Activity

Li4.MS Category

Accomplishment

Li4.MS Category
Awareness

Li4.MS Category

Alignment

CHAPTER 9
THE BOOK – PART FOUR

This week we finish reviewing the book, "Cover Me". We do this book review with the same mindset we learned from the introduction to the Song and the review of the movie. We are looking for "the hope of perfect love" in the story. We want to learn about this family and see what we can take away into our own lives.

WEEK 9 – THE BOOK PART FOUR
Remembering that this is a Study Guide with the goal of applying what we learn to our lives, we want to revisit our process (Li4.MS) from last week. Let's see how we did.

Let's each share about the items we recorded in Activity. Anyone want to be first?

Okay, great. And how did we do with Accomplishment? Did we get it done – Yes-No-Sort of?

So, what are you Aware of now that you had that Activity planned and the result in Accomplishment? Even if we did not do it, what did "not doing it" speak to you personally?

Finally, now that you have been through that Activity, Accomplishment, Awareness cycle, is there any Alignment you want to make for yourself going forward. Keep it simple. Maybe picture it in your mind as you write it down.

Great! Now to the book, "Cover Me".

We will be reviewing chapters numbered 12-15, when we meet. Be sure to read these ahead of time and record your responses to the questions here. It is these questions that we will be discussing when we meet. If anyone has a passage they would like us to read out loud, then let's do that. It is a great way to show how we interpret what is being said.

Make notes below of anything that catches your attention, especially as it relates to life and our own journey towards the hope for perfect love.

CHAPER 12 – Timing Is Everything
        ANSWER BEFORE WE MEET
What is the overall tone you pick up from this segment?

Record the relationships you see. What do we learn from the characters about these relationships?

What do you think of the agreement Benny made happen to catch Jimmy off guard?

Does reading this segment make you want to read more of the book?

What do you think the characters are thinking about the hope of perfect love, if anything, as this segment ends?

DISCUSS AND WRITE RESPONSES DURING MEEETING

So, what did you think? Can you relate to this experience of Michael's with his attorney? Did you ever have an experience where you find that there seems to be a series of events just falling in place? How did that impact you?

Let's take that thought and what we made note of in our first segment. This week, is there anything we saw that ties to the hope of perfect love for you? If so, what Activity can you do this week to implement something about it in your life, as an FP1. If you did not have anything that you related to, what can you come up with as an Activity for implementing an FP1 this week? Let's write those down. Is there an FP2? Write that down as well. And it is okay to have more than one of each. Again, make them realistic.

Make notes below of anything that catches your attention, especially as it relates to life and our own journey towards the hope for perfect love.

CHAPER 13 – Times Change - Everything
ANSWER BEFORE WE MEET
What is the overall tone you pick up from this segment?

Record the relationships you see. What do we learn from the characters about these relationships?

What do you think about Michael's presentation to Jimmy of the details he had discovered?

Does reading this segment make you want to read more of the book?

What do you think the characters are thinking about the hope of perfect love, if anything, as this segment ends?

DISCUSS AND WRITE RESPONSES DURING MEEETING

So, what did you think? Have you ever had someone try to deceive you only to have God expose their deeds?   How did it go?

Let's take that thought and what we made note of in our first

segment. This week, is there anything we saw that ties to the hope of perfect love for you? If so, what Activity can you do this week to implement something about it in your life, as an FP1. If you did not have anything that you related to, what can you come up with as an Activity for implementing an FP1 this week? Let's write those down. Is there an FP2? Write that down as well. And it is okay to have more than one of each. Again, make them realistic.

Make notes below of anything that catches your attention, especially as it relates to life and our own journey towards the hope for perfect love.

CHAPER 14 – The Sale Of A Lifetime
ANSWER BEFORE WE MEET
What is the overall tone you pick up from this segment?

Record the relationships you see. What do we learn from the characters about these relationships?

What do you think about the way the Old Man shows up? Who do you think he is?

Does reading this segment make you want to read more of the book?

What do you think the characters are thinking about the hope of perfect love, if anything, as this segment ends?

DISCUSS AND WRITE RESPONSES DURING MEEETING

So, what did you think? Ever have someone show up in a dream and then in real life? How did it go?

Let's take that thought and what we made note of in our first segment. This week, is there anything we saw that ties to the hope of perfect love for you? If so, what Activity can you do this week to implement something about it in your life, as an FP1. If you did not have anything that you related to, what can you come up with as an

Activity for implementing an FP1 this week? Let's write those down. Is there an FP2? Write that down as well. And it is okay to have more than one of each. Again, make them realistic.

Make notes below of anything that catches your attention, especially as it relates to life and our own journey towards the hope for perfect love.

CHAPER 15 – Vacation At Last
ANSWER BEFORE WE MEET
What is the overall tone you pick up from this segment?

Record the relationships you see. What do we learn from the characters about these relationships?

What do you think about how Michael pulled it all together? And what you think of the Ranger and the practice of keeping the fires lit for guests.

Does reading this segment make you want to read more of the book?

What do you think the characters are thinking about the hope of perfect love, if anything, as this segment ends?

DISCUSS AND WRITE RESPONSES DURING MEEETING

So, what did you think? Did Michael learn anything good? Did he dream something, or experience it, or both? Would you like this type of encounter with God, or have you had something like this? How did it go?

Let's take that thought and what we made note of in our first segment. This week, is there anything we saw that ties to the hope of perfect love for you? If so, what Activity can you do this week to implement something about it in your life, as an FP1. If you did not have anything that you related to, what can you come up with as an Activity for implementing an FP1 this week? Let's write those down.

Is there an FP2? Write that down as well. And it is okay to have more than one of each. Again, make them realistic.

Notes:

Li4.MS Category
Activity

Li4.MS Category

Accomplishment

Li4.MS Category

Awareness

Li4.MS Category

Alignment

CHAPTER 10
THE SONG – PART TWO AND SUMMARY

This week we will revisit where this journey started by reviewing the Song. We will also discuss our final application of the things we learned from the last four chapters of the Book. We will also discuss the overall time we have spent together, and complete our segments from the LI4.MS segments, summarizing what we did, what we learned, what we now know that maybe we did not know quite as well before, and what we want to do about it in our own lives. We are looking for "the hope of perfect love" in the story in these three different media. We want to find a way to align ourselves to that same hope of perfect love more each day.

WEEK 10 – THE SONG PART TWO
Remembering that this is a Study Guide with the goal of applying what we learn to our lives, we want to revisit our process (Li4.MS) from last week. Let's see how we did.

Let's each share about the items we recorded in Activity. Anyone want to be first?

Okay, great. And how did we do with Accomplishment? Did we get it done – Yes-No-Sort of?

So, what are you Aware of now that you had that Activity planned and the result in Accomplishment? Even if we did not do it, what did "not doing it" speak to you personally?

Finally, now that you have been through that Activity, Accomplishment, Awareness cycle, is there any Alignment you want to make for yourself going forward. Keep it simple. Maybe picture it in your mind as you write it down.

Great! Now to the song, "Cover Me".
We will be watch and listen to the lyric video one more time.

Make notes below of anything that catches your attention, especially things that tie to everything we have gone through so far.

What is there that you heard this time that after seeing and studying both the movie and the book, stand out? Is there anything in particular in the song that reminded you of the movie? Is there anything in particular in the song that reminded you of the book?

WEEK 10 – SUMMARY

We will end the day later with one more listen to the Song. Now we want to take a look at all that we have recorded.

Were there any planned Activity items that struck you as really important when you first planned them? If so, go to the Activity page for this chapter and write down the top three that come to mind. Remember, these were the planned activities, not necessarily what you actually did. We will get to the Accomplishment items next.

Does anyone have anything to share from these items that they planned?

Were there any Accomplishment items that struck you as really different or important when you did them? If so, go to the Accomplishment page for this chapter and write down the top three that come to mind. Remember, these were the actions that you actually took, maybe not planned. We will get to the Awareness items next.

Does anyone have anything to share from these items that they actually Accomplished?

Were there any planned Awareness items that struck you as really important, and possibly unexpected, when you first planned them? If so, go to the Awareness page in this chapter and write down the top three that come to mind. Remember, these were the planned activities, not necessarily what you actually did. We will get to the Alignment items next.

Does anyone have anything to share from these items that they gained an Awareness from during this time together?

Now we are coming to the focus of our ten weeks together. We started the journey with a heart toward the hope of perfect love. We expressed the idea that there are two focal points. Focal Point 1 – Love God with all your heart, soul, and mind. Focal Point 2 – Love your neighbor as yourself. Take a few minutes to first write FP1 or FP2 next to each of the items you listed in the Chapter 10 pages we just worked on. Then review the Alignment items you made over these weeks. Try to find the top three important ones to you in both the FP1 and FP2 categories.

Does anyone have anything to share from these items that they gained an Alignment items from this time together?

We have come to the end of our time together. But we are not at the end of the process of our drive towards the hope of perfect love. That is our walk with God – always every day. Let's commit to two things. First, let's each take the time everyday to walk out loving God with everything in us. And after that, let's share with others.

This is very important to us at the time this is originally written. It is also forever important. With the Song, the Book , or the Movie in your hand (not all three at the same time), strike up a conversation with someone that you may have wanted to share your faith with, or even a stranger that you may connect with in some way. Ask them to listen, read, or watch. And then when you get together to get it back, ask them what they thought. If they want to know more, you have a 10 week process you can walk them through, right?

Cover Me Movement is us. We make the difference. We CAN change the world...

Notes:

Li4.MS Category

Activity

Li4.MS Category

Accomplishment

Li4.MS Category
Awareness

Li4.MS Category

Alignment

ABOUT THE AUTHOR

Dr. Mark A. Smith served as a consultant and trainer to business for 25+ years. Each has also been faculty at local, regional, and international colleges and universities, focusing on Cognitive Science, his area of expertise. In 2012 God began to shift his focus and eventually his career to multi-mediated presentation.

Today he is an author of books, a writer-producer-director of feature length film, documentaries, and television. And he still writes poetry and songs. Combining all these skill sets he now works to help people learn more about the hope of a perfect love, for themselves and those around them.

And he wanted to tell everyone, he himself is on the path of learning. He hopes you will join him!